From
MORMON
ILLUSION

To

*GOD'S
LOVE*

# From MORMON ILLUSION

## To GOD'S LOVE

### Floyd C. McElveen

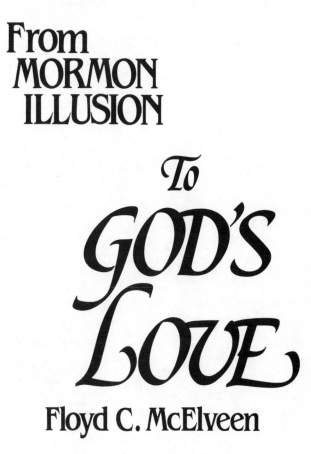

# INTRODUCTION

I write this book, by God's grace, on the authority of His written word, the Bible, the true "Testimony of the Holy Ghost," and His living Word within my heart, the Lord Jesus Christ. I believe He has prompted me to write this book.

After much prayer and study, I am doing for the Mormons exactly what I would hope they would do for me if the situation were reversed. God helping me, to the best of my ability, I am obeying His clear command to "speak the truth in love." May God's love be the anesthetic that makes the truth bearable. May He in His love bind up the broken hearts this may break. If I did not believe the exposure of these truths absolutely necessary to reach many or most Mormons for Christ, I would never, never do it. If I did not honestly believe the stakes are higher than life or death, even eternal heaven or eternal hell, I would not do it. If I did not believe the Lord Jesus Christ in His great love for these dear people, and millions influenced by them, was leading me to expose these painful truths, I would not do it. If I did not love Mormons, really, really care for where they spend eternity, I would not do it. May God grant that those who read this booklet read it all the way through to the very end. May He "renew their minds" and "open the eyes of their understanding."

This booklet is written to reach Mormons, and others also, for the Biblical Lord Jesus Christ. It is also written to inform those who do not know what Mormonism really is, and to help them to share these facts, and the clear way of salvation, with others. Without God, it is nothing. By God's grace, I pray He will use it mightily to reach thousands to His glory.

Because of the supreme importance of the material in this book, and the simple, clear, thorough presentation of salvation it gives, I believe it should be placed in the hands of every Mormon everywhere. I believe it should also be available to all who work with Mormons, or who are influenced by Mormonism.

We thank God with all our hearts for the right of Mormons to be Mormons, atheists to be atheists, Baptists to be Baptists, etc. and the right to worship in complete freedom. As Americans, we would defend this cherished right to the death. That is not the issue. However, our hearts cry out for those who, as in Jim Jones' cult, did not honestly face the truth about Jim Jones and his unbiblical life and doctrines. Instead they hid behind the consistent cry of the cults, "Why are you persecuting us?" "You took what he said out of context!" "They persecuted Jesus and said false things about Him too!"

The difference is that the things exposed about Jim Jones were true, not false, and motivated by love, not hate. Yet his followers ignored the truth and followed him to their doom. Just so, what we say about Mormonism is true, not false, and motivated by love, not hate. We pray God will cause Mormons to listen.

God loves Mormons, and so must we. Christ died for all of us. With that in mind, I introduce you to . . . "From Mormon Illusion to God's Love."

# PART I

# BEHIND THE IMAGE

## 1. DID YOU KNOW THAT THERE ARE MEN ON THE MOON? JOSEPH SMITH, THE MORMON PROPHET, SAID SO!

Quoting Joseph Smith, "The inhabitants of the moon are more of a uniform size than the inhabitants of the earth, being about 6 feet in height. They dress very much like the Quaker style and are quite general in style, or in the one fashion of dress. They live to be very old; coming generally near a thousand years." Huntington Library, San Marino, California, from the Journal of Oliver B. Huntington, Vol. 2, pg. 166. Claim repeated in Mormon church publication, "The Young Woman's Journal," published by the Young Ladies' Mutual Improvement Associations of Zion, 1892, Vol. 3, pg. 263-264.

## 2. DID YOU KNOW THERE IS LIFE ON THE SUN? BRIGHAM YOUNG, THE MORMON PROPHET, SAID SO!

"So it is with regard to the inhabitants of the Sun. Do you think there is any life there? No question about it; it was not made in vain." Journal of Discourses, Vol. 13, pg. 271. Brigham Young also said, "I have never yet preached a sermon and sent it out to the children of men that they may not call Scripture. Let me have the privilege of correcting a sermon, and it is as good Scripture as they deserve." J. D., Vol. 13, pg. 95. See also pg. 264.

### 3. DID YOU KNOW THAT NO MAN CAN ENTER HEAVEN WITHOUT THE CONSENT OF JOSEPH SMITH? BRIGHAM YOUNG SAID SO!

"No man or woman in this dispensation will ever enter the celestial kingdom of God without the consent of Joseph Smith!" Journal of Discourses, Vol. 7, pg. 289.

### 4. DID YOU KNOW THAT ALL WHO DO NOT ABIDE IN THE COVENANT OF POLYGAMY ARE DAMNED? JOSEPH SMITH SAID SO.

"For behold, I reveal unto you a new and EVER-LASTING covenant (polygamy), and if ye abide not that covenant, then are ye damned." Doctrine and Covenants 132:4. (Read chapter and context.)

### 5. DID YOU KNOW THAT THE ONLY WAY TO BECOME A GOD IS TO HAVE MORE THAN ONE WIFE? BRIGHAM YOUNG SAID SO!

"The only men who become Gods, even the Sons of God, are those who enter into polygamy." Journal of Discourses, Vol. 11, pg. 269; Vol. 3, pg. 266.

### 6. DID YOU KNOW THAT THERE WAS A TIME WHEN GOD WAS NOT GOD? JOSEPH SMITH SAID SO!

". . . I am going to tell you how God came to be God. We have imagined and supposed that God was God from all eternity. I will refute that idea, and take away the veil so that you may see." "Teachings of Prophet Joseph Smith," Deseret News Press, 1958, pg. 345. Also, the King Follett Discourse.

## 7. DID YOU KNOW THAT GOD WAS A MAN BEFORE HE BECAME GOD, AND HAD TO WORK, ATTAIN, EARN HIS WAY TO GODHOOD? DID YOU KNOW THAT MEN, "MORMON MEN ONLY" CAN BECOME GODS?

"Articles of Faith," James E. Talmage, pg. 430, 1952 edition. See also Lorenzo Snow & Milton Hunter. Quote, "As man is, God once was: As God is man may be." (This is in *total contradiction* to Isaiah 43:10B: ". . . Before me there was no God formed, neither shall there be after me." and to Psalm 90:2B: ". . . *From* everlasting *to* everlasting, *thou art God*.) The Mormon God is still progressing, and the God Mormons believed fathered Him has progressed more than the God of this world. In fact, many Gods may be farther along in progression. This makes the Mormon God a lesser, incomplete God, one among many, not the one true God of all possible "worlds" and "universes," like the Biblical God of the Christians. Incidentally, the Mormon God, as distinct from the God of the Bible, is not omnipresent. He is limited in space and time by a physical body.

The Bible says God is a spirit, not God HAS a spirit. I *have* a basketball. I am NOT a basketball. In Luke 24:39B, Jesus said, "A spirit *hath not* flesh and bones, as ye see Me have." This is why the Bible says no man has seen God, though He sometimes appeared in the form of a man, and manifested Himself in the flesh to men in the person of Jesus Christ (I Tim. 3:16). See also John 1:18; I John 4:12; I Tim. 6:16.

The Mormon God is not all-powerful, or Almighty, as

the Biblical God is declared to be. There are other Gods, or at least a God from which He came, farther in progression than He is. They, too, have power, possibly even greater than His, over "universes" of their own. Obviously, the Mormon God and the Biblical God are two different Gods!

## 8. DID YOU KNOW THAT MORMONS BELIEVE THERE ARE MANY GODS? JOSEPH SMITH SAID SO!

"And the Gods ordered, saying: Let the waters under the heaven be gathered together in one place . . .; . . . and the Gods pronounced the dry land, earth: . . .: and the Gods saw that they were obeyed." Pearl of Great Price, Abraham 4:9, 10. Also: "If we should take a million of worlds like this and number their particles we should find that there are more Gods than there are particles of matter in those worlds." Mormon Apostle Orson Pratt, Journal of Discourses, Vol. 2, 1854 (1966 reprint), pg. 345. (See Isaiah 44:34!)

## 9. DID YOU KNOW GOD HAS MANY WIVES, AND THAT MORMONS HAVE A MOTHER GOD? BRIGHAM YOUNG, AMONG OTHERS, SAID SO, AS DID APOSTLE ORSON PRATT.

"We have now shown that GOD THE FATHER had a plurality of wives, one or more being in eternity, by whom He begat our spirits as well as the spirit of Jesus His first born . . ." "The Seer," pg. 172. See also "Mormon Doctrine," by Apostle Bruce McConkie for information on a Heavenly Mother, pgs. 516, 517. Also, "Gospel Through the Ages," pg. 98, Milton R. Hunter.

## 10. DID YOU KNOW THAT ADAM WAS GOD? THE ONLY GOD WITH WHOM WE HAVE TO DO? BRIGHAM YOUNG SAID SO . . . MANY TIMES IN MANY PLACES FOR MANY YEARS!!!!

"When our father Adam came into the Garden of Eden, he came into it with a celestial body, and brought Eve, one of his wives, with him. He helped to make and organize this world. He is Michael the Archangel, the Ancient of Days about whom holy men have written and spoken—He is our father and our God, and *the only God with whom we have to do.*" Journal of Discourses, Vol. 1, pgs. 50, 51, from sermon Brigham Young gave April 9, 1852. To be sure he was not misunderstood on his clear teaching that Adam is God, Brigham Young said the same thing in even stronger and clearer language two years later on February 19, 1854. He taught the same thing in 1857 (J. D., Vol. 5, pg. 331), and he was still teaching and preaching that Adam was God as late as 1873, as Mormon publications show.

## 11. DID YOU KNOW THAT MANY MORMONS HAD A "TESTIMONY OF THE HOLY GHOST," THAT BRIGHAM YOUNG'S TEACHING ON ADAM BEING GOD WAS TRUE?

Tens of thousands of Mormons came to accept this doctrine as true, and it was held by the Mormon church as truth for about 50 years. Apostle Orson Pratt did not believe the doctrine at first and was in danger of excommunication for a while. Read now the testimony of some leading and devout Mormons. "Concerning the doctrine that Adam is our Father and God . . . the prophet and Apostle Brigham has declared it, and that is the word of the Lord." F. D. Richards, Millenial Star, August 26,

1854, Vol. 16, pg. 534. Following his leader Brigham Young, George Q. Cannon taught, ". . . Jesus is Jehovah," also that "Adam is his Father and our God." "Diary Journal of Abraham H. Cannon," June 23, 1889, Vol. 11, pg. 39. Mormon Edward W. Tullige wrote, "Adam is our Father and God. He is God of the earth. So says Brigham Young." "The Women of Mormondom," 1877, pgs. 79, 179, 196, 197. Mormon Hosea Stout wrote, "Another meeting this evening. President B. Young taught that Adam was the Father of Jesus and the only God to us." "Diary of Hosea Stout," April 9, 1852, Vol. 2, pg. 435. Many of these Mormons *heard* Brigham Young and recorded and believed what he said about Adam being God!!!

## 12. DID YOU KNOW THAT PRESIDENT SPENCER KIMBALL AND THOUSANDS OF OTHER MORMONS NOW HAVE A "TESTIMONY OF THE HOLY GHOST," THAT THE ADAM-GOD DOCTRINE IS FALSE, AND NOW DENY THAT BRIGHAM YOUNG EVER TAUGHT THIS DOCTRINE?

President Spencer Kimball said in "Church News," October 9, 1976, "We warn you against the dissemination of doctrines which are not according to the scriptures and which are ALLEGED to have been taught by some of the General Authorities of past generations. Such, for instance, is the Adam-God THEORY. We denounce that theory and hope that everyone will be cautioned against this and other kinds of FALSE DOCTRINE." (Question: If one accepts Brigham Young as a prophet of God, and therefore accepts his Adam-God revelation, would that not admit that Spencer W. Kimball is a false prophet misleading honest but confused

LDS people? If one accepts Spencer W. Kimball as a prophet of God, would that not indicate that Brigham Young was a false prophet, misleading sincere but deluded LDS people? This illustrates graphically why turning away from light God has already given in His Word, and "praying for more light," depending on the subjective feelings of the "Testimony of the Holy Ghost," rather than the clear word of God, is not and cannot be God's way of determining truth. The Bereans, more noble than those in Thessalonica, "searched the scriptures daily, whether those things were so." Acts 17:11.)

Look where the "Testimony of the Holy Ghost" has led Mormon leaders and Mormons in general. Millions of people in hundreds of religions and cults have prayed for light, are honest and sincere, and have a testimony that they have the truth. Hundreds of millions of Protestants have a "Testimony of the Holy Ghost," that they are right, as do millions of Catholics. Yet none of this means anything unless what they believe squares with the Bible. Gal. 1:8, "But though we, or an angel from heaven, preach any other gospel unto you than that which we have preached unto you, let him be accursed."

**To sum up:** To believe that Brigham Young was a prophet of God and accept his Adam-God revelation, is to admit that the present-day "prophet" Spencer W. Kimball and the Mormon church are false. To DENY the Adam-God doctrine is to deny the prophet Brigham Young, and admit that Brigham Young and the Mormon church are false! To rely on the "Testimony of the Holy Ghost," as thousands of Mormons did to *believe* the Adam-God doctrine, and then to rely on the "Testimony of the Holy Ghost," to DENY the Adam-God doctrine, as Spencer W. Kimball and thousands of Mormons now do, is to show the total unreliability of what Mormons mistakenly CALL the "Testimony of the Holy Ghost," (feelings, burning in the bosom, etc.). The only fully reliable, authoritative, God-endorsed "Testimony of the Holy Ghost," is the Bible, the Word of God, written by men of God inspired by the Holy Ghost. No experience, testimony, feeling, conviction, burning in the bosom, or vision is a "Testimony of the Holy Ghost," if it contradicts the Bible, the Word of God. The Holy Ghost (more properly, Holy Spirit) does not contradict the Holy Ghost!

### 13. DID YOU KNOW THAT, AFTER YEARS OF DENIAL AND COVER-UP BY MORMON AUTHORITIES, LDS APOSTLE BRUCE R. McCONKIE HAS NOW CONFESSED THAT BRIGHAM YOUNG TAUGHT THE ADAM-GOD DOCTRINE?

"Yes, President Young did teach that Adam was the father of our spirits, and all the related things that the cultist ascribe to him. . . ." Letter to Mr. Eugene England, February 19, 1981. Read the full letter in context as recorded in "LDS Apostle Confesses Brigham Young Taught Adam-God Doctrine," Modern Microfilm Company, P.O. Box 1884, Salt Lake City, Utah, 84110. Apostle McConkie went on the *deny* the doctrine he admitted Brigham taught. Read it for yourself, to be fair to Apostle Bruce R. McConkie.

### 14. DID YOU KNOW THAT JESUS CHRIST WAS NOT VIRGIN BORN? THAT JESUS WAS FATHERED BY ADAM-GOD IN PHYSICAL SEX RELATIONS WITH MARY? BRIGHAM YOUNG SAID SO!

"Jesus Christ was not begotten by the Holy Ghost." (This is in direct contradiction of Matt. 1:20B: ". . . for

that which is conceived in her *is of the Holy Ghost.*")
Brigham Young, Journal of Discourses, Vol. 1, pgs. 50,
51. Also, after having declared Adam as our Father and
God and the only God with whom we have to do, in his
April 9, 1852 sermon, Brigham Young went on to identify
Adam as the Father of Jesus, a fact recorded by Journal
of Discourses, Vol. 1, pgs. 50, 51 and by many diaries and
journals of leading Mormons of that day, who heard him
give the message. Brigham Young forever clarified exactly what he meant on *February 19, 1854,* nearly two
years after his initial Adam-God sermon. Not only did
he reassert that Adam was God, but he also reasserted
unmistakeably that Adam was the Father of Jesus
Christ, in the actual, direct, physical sex act, with
Mary, in begetting Him. "Who did beget Him? His
father, and His father is our God, and the FATHER OF
OUR SPIRITS, and he is the framer of the body, the God
and Father of our Lord Jesus Christ. Who is He? He is
Father Adam." Brigham Young Paper, February 18,
1854, call number MSF 219 # 81, Church Historians Of-
fice, Salt Lake City, Utah.

15. **DID YOU KNOW THAT GOD HAD, OR IS
HAVING, PHYSICAL SEX RELATIONS WITH
HIS WIFE OR WIVES, TO PROVIDE SPIRITS
TO INHABIT EVERY BODY THAT HAS
BEEN, IS NOW, OR EVER WILL BE UPON
THIS EARTH?**

Many Mormon sources are involved in this teaching,
including Orson Pratt, "The Seer," pg. 172, Joseph
Fielding Smith in "Doctrine of Salvation," and many
others. If God fathered a child every second day and
night, 24 hours a day, it would take him 250 years to
father 1 billion children. It would take him 1,000 years
and more to father the present population of the earth at

1 second per wife (and the population of the earth is expected to double in a few decades, not to mention the billions that have lived before and may come later!!!). If God spent 5 minutes per wife, day and night, even for the present population alone, it would take him over 300,000 years to furnish spirits for just the population we now have. But this is not counting the 9 months pregnancy, the raising of the family, and the myriad of other tasks in running the Universe; now we go into uncounted billions of years! The Mormon answer that Gid did much of of this "fathering" in eternity, before the "organization" of the earthly universe, seems very weak. Spirits, according to big family Mormons, are yearning for bodies to go through this "probation" period, and advance or progress, possibly even into Godhood. The body is essential. How torturous to father them and keep them waiting for millions and billions of years! Seems very unlike a God of love, or at least a very unlikely way of doing things. We cannot but wonder about this intense preoccupation with sex, many wives, etc. both in regard to God, and Mormon's exaltation as "gods" with wives and a planet of their own to populate by sexual liaisons. Does it not sound far more like the phallic religions of paganism, than the Bible Christianity of Jesus Christ? But I honestly do not wish to be unfair. I care for Mormons . . . very much. Dear reader, what do YOU think?

16. **DID YOU KNOW THAT JOSEPH SMITH WAS TRIED IN 1826, FOR FRAUD, AND CONVICTED? (IN A CRYSTAL-GAZING, FORTUNE-FINDING, "GLASS-LOOKER" DECEPTION OF AN OLD MAN, JOSIAH STOWELL, CONCERNING FINDING LOST PROPERTY AND GOLD TREASURES ON HIS LAND—FOR A PRICE, OF COURSE.)**

Joseph Smith's method was to put a stone in his hat and put his face in the hat, the same process strangely, according to Book of Mormon witness David Whitmer, in, "An Address to All Believers in Christ," pg. 12, by which Joseph Smith translated the Book of Mormon! (It is very difficult to determine the real value of the "golden plates" Smith said he found containing the Book of Mormon in "Reformed Egyptian," since they were seldom, if ever, present or used when Smith was translating.) Why would God preserve those plates for centuries and then lead Joseph Smith to them if they were virtually useless?? (See No. 22.)

Note that this was 6 years after Joseph Smith claimed to have had the *First Vision in 1820, on which foundation Mormonism rests. Dr. Hugh Nibley, Mormon Scholar, said, on pg. 142 of "The Myth Makers," that it would be a "devastating blow" to Joseph Smith, if such a court record could be found. It was found . . . the original court record, by Wesley P. Walters, in Chenango County Courthouse, New York, July 28, 1971!!! Anyone who wishes can see or obtain a photostatic copy of this original court record from several sources, one of them being Modern Microfilm Company, in Salt Lake City. *(The First Vision is where Joseph Smith claimed to have seen the Father and the Son at age 14, and this is the foundation of Mormonism. Yet other versions of this First Vision, long suppressed, have surfaced, wherein Smith gives totally contradictory accounts of his age, 14, 16, and 17, the date of the Vision, 1820 or 1823, and who and what he saw. Brigham Young, close confidant and later Mormon Living Prophet and President said, "The Lord did not come . . . but He did send His angel to this same obscure person, Joseph Smith jun. . . ." Journal of Discourses," Vol. 2, pg. 171. After supposedly seeing the Father and the Son in 1820, at age 14, Joseph Smith is quoted in the Mormon Messenger and Advocate, Vol. 1, pgs. 78, 79, as actually having the Vision in 1823, at age 17. Joseph Smith is quoted, at the age of 17, as wondering, "if a Supreme Being did exist". . . !!! If indeed there was a Vision, it obviously did not come from God! If he had seen God at age 14, as Mormons now insist, and as the official "First Vision" states—he would not be wondering "if a Supreme Being did exist" at age 17!!

## 17. DID YOU KNOW THAT JOSEPH SMITH GOT EVERY LETTER AND EVERY WORD OF HIS TRANSLATION OF THE BOOK OR MORMON DIRECT FROM GOD WITH ABSOLUTELY NO POSSIBILITY OF ANY MISTAKE WHATSOEVER?

So said Joseph Smith, David Whitmer, and Joseph F. Smith. Joseph Smith said, after the printing of the Book of Mormon, that it was the "most correct of any book on earth." Smith, "History of the Church," Vol. 4, pg. 461. Joseph F. Smith, sixth president of the Mormon Church, declared, "Joseph did not render the writing on the gold plates into the English language in his own style of language as many people believe, but every word and every letter was given to him by the gift and power of God." WHY THEN HAVE THERE BEEN SOME 4,000 CHANGES IN GRAMMAR, PUNCTUATION AND WORD STRUCTURE IN THE "PERFECT" BOOK OF MORMON? One can buy the 1830 reproduction of the original Book of Mormon and can see these changes for themselves, by comparing it with the modern Book of Mormon.

## 18. DID YOU KNOW THAT JOSEPH SMITH FINISHED A COMPLETE TRANSLATION OF

## THE BIBLE, "JOSEPH SMITH'S INSPIRED VERSION OF THE BIBLE," IN WHICH HE ADDED TO THE BOOK OF REVELATION?

". . . We this day finished the translation of the Scriptures . . ." "Having finished the translation of the Bible, a few hours since." "Times and Seasons," Vol. 6, pg. 802, also "History of the Church, Period 1", Joseph Smith, Vol. 1, pgs. 368, 369. Revelation 22:18, 19 pronounces God's curse of utter doom for those who add to or take from this book (and/or His total word).

## 19. DID YOU KNOW THAT MANY OF JOSEPH SMITH'S PROPHECIES FAILED?

Prophecy 1. David Patten to go on a mission in the Spring, D&C 114:1. He did not, he was killed before Spring. False.

Prophecy 2. New Jerusalem and its Temple to be built in Missouri in Joseph Smith's generation. It was not. False.

Prophecy 3. Brethren to go to Toronto, Canada, and there assuredly sell the copyright to the Book of Mormon. They did not. False.

Prophecy-revelation 4. There are men on the Moon. False.

God's test for a prophet was very simple and very clear, so that no one need be deceived by a false prophet. Deut. 18:20-22, "But the prophet which shall presume to speak a word in my name which I have not commanded him to speak, or that shall speak in the name of other gods, *even that prophet shall die.* And if thou say in thine heart, How shall we know the word which the Lord hath not spoken? When a prophet speaketh in the name of the Lord, if the thing follow not, nor came to pass, that is the thing which the Lord hath not spoken but the prophet hath spoken it presumptuously; thou shalt not be afraid of him." Doctrine and Covenants 114:1, David Patten is told to settle up his business to "perform a mission unto me next Spring, in company with others, even twelve including himself, to testify of my name and bear glad tidings unto all the world." This prophecy was given April 17, 1838. On October 25, 1838, David Patten was shot and killed. The prophecy was false. He did *not* go on a mission "next Spring." Doctrine and Covenants 84:1-5, a revelation given in September 1832, saying that New Jerusalem and its TEMPLE are to be built in Missouri in *this generation*. ". . . for verily *this generation* shall not all pass away until an house shall be built unto the Lord." We know for a fact that Joseph Smith meant the generation that was then alive when he spoke, and many of the faithful declared that very fact, and Joseph Smith never at any time corrected them. Again and again Mormon apostles, many of them who heard the message and were in close contact with Joseph Smith, declared that Joseph meant exactly what he said; the current generation of Mormons alive when Joseph Smith gave the prophecy would not die before the fulfillment of the prophecy. See Journal of Discourses, Vol. 9, pg. 71; Vol. 10, pg. 344; Vol. 13, pg. 362. Apostle Orson Pratt stated conclusively: "The Latter-day Saints just as much expect to receive a fulfillment of that promise, *during the generation that was in existence in 1832* as they expect that the sun will rise and set tomorrow. Why? Because God cannot lie. He will fulfill all His promises." Pratt was speaking of the New Jerusalem, Temple prophecy. (See full statement, Journal of Discourses, Vol. 9, pg. 71.) The City was NOT built, the Temple was NOT built in "this generation." The prophecy was obviously false.

Joseph Smith prophesied that the brethren should go to Toronto, Canada, and that they would sell the copyright of the Book of Mormon. They went, but could not sell the book, and called Joseph Smith to account. Do you know what Joseph Smith said? "Some revelations are of God, some are of men, and some are of the devil." Apparently, he couldn't tell the difference! Source: "An Address to All Believers in Christ," David Whitmer.

Unfortunately for our Mormon friends, all Mormon "living prophets" have the same problem. Apostle Parley Pratt prophesied in 1838 that in 50 years there would not be an unbelieving Gentile upon this continent. Heber C. Kimball prophesied that Brigham Young would become President of the United States. Oliver B. Huntington was told in his Patriarchal blessing, given by the father of Joseph the Prophet, that he would preach the gospel to the inhabitants of the MOON! (Recorded in the diary of Oliver B. Huntington, Utah State Historical Society, and also in the Huntington Library in San Marino, California. Also recorded in the "Mormon's Young Women's Journal," Vol. 3, No. 6 of 1892.) Obviously, Joseph Smith and other Mormon prophets were false prophets! (Deut. 13:1-5 gives further evidence that Joseph Smith was a false prophet.)

God asks one thing of us, beloved friends . . . that we be honest with the facts. These prophecies were false, and there are many more like them. God says this is how we determine a false prophet. We ask our Mormon friends to please be honest with God and with themselves. It does no good to lash out at the truth (or at me), it will not change one fact. We say to our Mormon friends, "God loves you, and wants you to know the truth, and so do I." Your reaction may well determine your eternal destiny.

20. **DID YOU KNOW THE "BOOK OF ABRAHAM" AND ITS PURPORTED TRANSLATION FROM EGYPTIAN TO ENGLISH BY JOSEPH SMITH, HAS BEEN DECLARED A FRAUD BY EVERY LEADING EGYPTOLOGIST THAT HAS EXAMINED IT?**

The "drawings" etc. in the Book of Abraham . . . Facsimile no. 1, taken by Smith from some papyri he purchased from one Michael H. Chandler (which was rediscovered in 1967), was declared by Joseph Smith to show the idolatrous priest of Elkenah attempting to offer Abraham upon the altar as a sacrifice. The four jars underneath were idolatrous gods, etc. The bird pictured was the "Angel of the Lord." Actually every Egyptologist (an expert in the Egyptian language and customs) who has examined the manuscript and Joseph Smith's translation, has claimed that it is actually an Egyptian funeral text from a few centuries before the birth of Christ, giving instructions to the embalmers! *All* agree Joseph Smith's translation is false. See "Mormonism, Shadow or Reality," Jerald and Sandra Tanner, chapter on "The Fall of the Book of Abraham." Two Egyptologists who replied to a request by Marvin Cowan for their statement on this matter where Prof. John A. Wilson and Richard A. Parker (University of Chicago and Brown University.)

*Professor Dee Jay Nelson, a Mormon Egyptologist, also examined the Book of Abraham, along with several renown Egyptologists. Prof. Nelson resigned from the Mormon Church when he and his fellow Egyptologist discovered Joseph Smith's Book of Abraham in the "Pearl of Great Price" to be an outright fraud. These Egyptologists, besides Nelson, were Richard A. Parker, Chairman of the Department of Egyptology at Brown University, and Klaus Baer, Associate Professor of Egyptology, University of Chicago's Oriental Institute.

---

*Although there may be some doubt as to Prof. Nelson's credentials, as the Tanner's have shown, he does have some expertise as an Egyptologist. Furthermore, the other Egyptologists are renowned experts with inpeccable credentials!!!

## 21. DID YOU KNOW THAT THERE WAS NO AGE OF METAL IN AMERICA FOR AT LEAST SIX CENTURIES AFTER JOSEPH SMITH CLAIMS THE BOOK OF MORMON PEOPLE FOUND VARIOUS METALS IN ABUNDANCE IN THE AMERICAS?

Jaredites, Lamanites, Nephthites, etc. used silver, gold, iron, steel, brass, copper, tools of metal, weapons of war, etc. lavishly, according to the Book of Mormon. Yet this is in direct contradiction to all archeological evidence. Not one reputable archeologist has ever found any evidence to support this claim. All facts declare this to be false. The Book of Mormon also lists 38 major cities existing in the Americas. Not ONE city site has EVER been found; by any archeologist, Mormon or otherwise! They simply never existed, except in Joseph Smith's imagination. Major city sites of the Bible, some much older, have easily been found and verified. Even the animals Joseph Smith's Book of Mormon claimed were in the Americas, such as cattle, swine, horses, etc. were not brought here until centuries later!!!

## 22. DID YOU KNOW THAT THE "GOLD PLATES" UPON WHICH THE BOOK OF MORMON WAS SUPPOSEDLY WRITTEN IN "REFORMED EGYPTIAN," WERE NOT USED AT ALL WHEN JOSEPH SMITH WAS TRANSLATING THE BOOK OF MORMON!!??

Emma Smith, Joseph's wife, and Oliver Cowdery, often acted as scribes to Joseph Smith as he translated. They, along with "witnesses" David Whitmer and Martin Harris, described in detail how Joseph Smith translated. He stuck his face in a hat with a stone in the hat ". . . something resembling parchment would appear."

Hieroglyphics would appear on the parchment, with the exact, perfect English interpretation underneath. Joseph Smith would read it, and Oliver Cowdery, or whoever was acting as scribe at that time, would write it. When correctly written, the hieroglyphics and its English interpretation would disappear. If not correctly written, the words of the parchment would remain until every letter, every character, every word was perfect, exactly as God gave it." (See David Whitmer, "An Address to All Believers in Christ.") Also corroborated by Emma Smith and the other "witnesses," Cowdery and Harris. THE GOLD PLATES WERE SELDOM, IF EVER, PRESENT. (IF THEY INDEED EXISTED) THEY WERE NEVER USED IN TRANSLATION! THEY WERE UTTERLY USELESS! Indeed,Oliver Cowdery, one of the three witnesses to the Book of Mormon, said, "I have sometimes had sessions of skepticism, in which I did seriously wonder whether the prophet and I were men in our sober senses when we would be translating from the plates through the Urim and Thummin (which the seer stone eventually came to be called), and THE PLATES NOT BE IN SIGHT AT ALL!" From "Defense in a Rehearsal of My Grounds for Separating Myself from the Latter Day Saints," Oliver Cowdery. Strangely enough, the three main witnesses to the Book of Mormon had to have an angel show them the plates, though supposedly in the custody of Joseph Smith, and saw the plates with the "eye of faith," as Harris and others said. Also, "by faith," as Doctrine and Covenants says in 17:5.

Now the eight witnesses "hefted" the plates, and Joseph Smith packed them great distances, once running a mile or so with them and once carrying them for three miles. This is remarkable, as Marvin Cowan shows in his book, "Mormon Claims Answered." The size of the plates was about 7 inches wide by 8 inches long, a little less thick than ordinary sheet tin, fastened by three rings running through the plates near one edge, making the book of plates nearly 6 inches thick. (See "Articles of Faith," Talmage, 262-263) Cowan says succinctly, ". . . gold weighs 1204.7256 pounds per cubic foot. Thus, 6 inches × 7 inches × 8 inches—336 inches or .19444. Cowan says succinctly, ". . . gold weighs 1204. 7256, pounds per cubic foot. Thus, 6 inches × 7 inches × 8 inches—336 cubic inches or .19444 cubic feet derived by dividing 336 by 12 cubed or 1728. When 1204. 7256 is multiplied by .19444 we see that the gold plates weighed about 234. 246845664 pounds." (Forget the confusing decimals, the gold plates weighed about 234 pounds.)

This, among other things listed, is what Mormons claim they have a "Testimony of the Holy Ghost," about, that it is true! The Biblical "Testimony of the Holy Ghost," is the WORD OF GOD! II Tim. 3:16: ". . . All Scripture is given by inspiration of God . . ." The Holy Ghost, or Holy Spirit, refers to the same person. The same Greek word is used and is sometimes translated Ghost, sometimes Spirit interchangeably. The "Testimony of the Holy Ghost," is first and foremost the written word, the Bible. No experience, testimony, feeling, burning in the bosom, conviction, vision, etc. which contradicts the written "Testimony of the Holy Ghost," the Bible, could possibly be from God. The only experience the true "Testimony of the Holy Ghost would ever give, is that which supports and corroborates the written Word of God. The Holy Ghost does not contradict the Holy Ghost. God is not the Author of Confusion.

23. **DID YOU KNOW THAT THE BOOK OF MORMON AND THE PEARL OF GREAT PRICE, ON THE ONE HAND, AND DOCTRINE AND COVENANTS, ON THE OTHER HAND, PLACE ADAM AND EVE AND THEIR DESCENDANTS ON THE OPPOSITE SIDES OF THE EARTH AT THE SAME TIME?!**

The one account places them in the Middle East, the other account says that the Garden of Eden and Adam and Eve were in Davies County, Missouri! (Summed up, documented, and compared in the fine little book, "Joseph and the Golden Plates," by Gordon H. Fraser.)

## 24. DID YOU KNOW THAT JOSEPH SMITH KICKED A MAN OUT OF THE CHURCH FOR PREACHING THE "FALSE AND CORRUPT DOCTRINE" OF POLYGAMY, WHEN HE WAS PRACTICING POLYGAMY HIMSELF?

Joseph Smith's revelation requiring polygamy was recorded in Doctrine and Covenants 132 on July 12, 1843. Yet Andrew Jensen, a Mormon Church Historian, lists 27 women who were married to Joseph Smith in "Historical Record," pgs. 233, 234. Other Mormon sources list that many and more, married to Joseph Smith for time and eternity. Several well-documented Mormon sources even admit that Joseph Smith also took other men's wives, and actually cohabitated with them. For accurate, thorough documentation from Mormon's own records, see "Mormonism, Shadow or Reality," by Jerald and Sandra Tanner, chapter on Plural Marriage. Also, while practicing polygamy themselves, though outwardly denying it, Joseph Smith and Hyrum Smith excommunicated Hiram Brown for ". . . Preaching polygamy, and other FALSE and CORRUPT doctrines." This notice was published in *Times and Seasons*, Vol. 5, pg. 72, on THURSDAY, FEBRUARY 1, 1844! It is just possible that some may see this as the act of a man who is deliberately deceptive, immoral, callous and cynical, and utterly dishonest. Others may view it in a "kinder" light. May God in His love help us all to be totally honest with the truth!

## 25. DID YOU KNOW THAT MORMON WOMEN'S HIGHEST EXALTATION SIMPLY BOILS DOWN TO BEING ETERNALLY PREGNANT???

On the other hand, anything less than "Highest Exaltation" and being eternally pregnant leaves the Mormon woman pretty much as an insignificant servant to those more "worthy." My heart really goes out to Mormon women. No wonder the suicide rate is increasing by leaps and bounds, no wonder so much severe depression and break-ups are being experienced in Mormon homes!

## 26. DID YOU KNOW THAT MORMONS DELIBERATELY VIOLATE GOD'S EXPRESS COMMAND FORBIDDING GENEOLOGIES?

I Tim. 1:4: . . . "Neither give heed to fables and endless geneologies." Titus 3:9, "AVOID foolish questions and GENEOLOGIES. . . ." Mormons do not realize they have fulfilled their purpose and are now FORBIDDEN!

## 27. DID YOU KNOW THAT MORMONS GLORY IN A PRIESTHOOD THAT IS DEAD, OVER, FINISHED AND TOTALLY NON-EXISTENT AS FAR AS AN OFFICIAL PRIESTHOOD IS CONCERNED IN THE NEW TESTAMENT CHURCH!?

1. Preists had one MAJOR purpose: To offer blood sacrifices UNTIL the Lamb of God, Jesus, came to shed His blood, ONCE FOR ALL!
2. There is no official Priesthood, or order of Priests in the New Testament church. This was DONE AWAY WITH when Christ shed His blood on Cal-

vary, and rose again. He now is our ONE AND ONLY HIGH PRIEST. No other priest is ever even so much as mentioned, in connection with the New Testament church, in decades of writing by the New Testament writers, as they wrote on the church. Not once is any priest whatsoever mentioned in the numerous times offices and officers of the church are mentioned. They are GONE! All such priests today are false priests however nice and sincere they may be! Their Authority is imagined, conferred on them by a bogus "Prophet." There are no priests since Pentecost in the true New Testament church. See Eph. 4:11.

3. ALL Christians are now declared to be priests unto God, with Christ as our one and only High Priest forever! Whatever do we need with official priests now? They were merely to give blood sacrifices and point to Jesus, until He came and shed His blood for us! (See I Peter 2:9, Rev. 1:4-6 and Heb. 7:21.)

28. **DID YOU KNOW GOD FORBIDS A CHURCH LEADER, BISHOP, ELDER, DEACON, BEING THE HUSBAND OR MORE THAN ONE WIFE? YET JOSEPH SMITH, BRIGHAM YOUNG, AND OTHER MORMON LEADERS HAD MORE THAN ONE WIFE, NULLIFYING ALL THEIR CLAIMS OF AUTHORITY FROM GOD FOR BOTH THEMSELVES AND THEIR SUCCESSORS!**

See I Tim. 1:1-12. True Christians get their authority from John 1:12, II Cor. 5:17-21, I Pet. 2:5—from the Word of God without (which is the Bible) and the Word of God within (which is Jesus).

## 29. DID YOU KNOW JESUS CHRIST WAS CRUCIFIED BECAUSE HE WAS A POLYGAMIST?

So claimed Jedeiah M. Grant, Second Counselor to Brigham Young. Journal of Discourses, Vol. 1, pg. 345, 346.

## 30. DID YOU KNOW THAT JESUS, LIKE GOD THE FATHER, HAD TO EARN PROGRESS, ATTAIN HIS WAY INTO GODHOOD? "WHAT THE MORMONS THINK OF CHRIST." Pg. 36.

Mormons believe Jesus is a God named Jehovah, God the Father is a completely separate God, one in purpose only with Jesus. God the Father's name is Elohim. Thus they undeniably have two Gods. (Not to mention the myriads of other "Gods" they believe exist . . . and not to mention that they still have Adam-God, "The only God with whom we have to do," to contend with. Plus many "exalted men" who have become "Gods".) The truth is, Jehovah and Elohim are names used interchangely, over and over again, for the ONE true God. Notice, for example, Deut. 6:4B; "The LORD (JEHOVAH) our God (Elohim) is one LORD: (JEHOVAH). Jesus is called Elohim, he is also called Jehovah. God the Father is called Elohim, he is also called JEHOVAH. This is because God the Father, God the Son, and God the Holy Spirit, $1 \times 1 \times 1 = 1$—one God! The Bible even speaks of the one God as "Jehovah-Elohim." It makes as little sense to try to separate these two names for God, and claim they represent separate Gods, and it does to separate Jehovah-jireh, Jehovah-rophe, Jehovah-M'Kaddesh, Jehovah-shalom, Jehovah-tsidkenu, or Jehovah-shamah, and say that each of these names—all used of God as descriptive attributes—that each stands for a separate God! El, and El-Shaddai, are other names used of the one true God in some special relationship to His people, NOT different Gods!

Just as space exists in height, length and breadth, *three* distinctions in *one* space, and just as *each* extended infinitely is *all there is of space,* and yet all three dimensions or distinctions are necessary, (or one could not even build a house), so it is with God the Father, God the Son, and God the Holy Spirit. One God, as space is one, with three distinct persons in the nature of the one True God. So, too, it is with time—past, present and future—three clear distinctions, yet time is absolutely ONE. God, being 3-in-1, and the Creator of this vast Universe naturally affixed His signature, 3-in-1, to the basic elements!

So then, Jesus Christ is God, and always has been and always will be! He is one in essence with the Father. NOTICE: The Bible says to know Jesus is to know God, to see Jesus is to see God, to believe in Jesus is to believe in God, to honor Jesus is to honor God, and to hate Jesus is to hate God. God is called the First and the Last. Jesus Christ is called the First and the Last. You simply cannot have TWO Firsts and Lasts in the ultimate sense this is used of God! Both are called the Almighty God. Jesus forgave sin, and the Bible says only God can forgive sin. Things that are said in the Old Testament about God the Father are said in the New Testament about Jesus. The Father God is called our Savior and Creator in the Old Testament. Jesus Christ is called our Savior and the Creator in the New Testament. An elementary rule of logic is that things equal to the same thing are equal to each other (if A equals B and B equals C, then A equals C). Jesus is thus declared to be God, as He claimed to be. No wonder Thomas called Jesus, "My Lord and my God!" John 20:28.

31. **DID YOU KNOW JOSEPH SMITH (AND OTHER MORMON OFFICIALS) ARE ON RECORD AS CALLING HIS THREE MAIN WITNESSES TO THE BOOK OF MORMON, "THIEVES AND LIARS!!" JOSEPH SMITH ALSO SAID, "DAVID WHITMER, OLIVER COWDERY, AND MARTIN HARRIS, ARE TOO MEAN TO MENTION, AND WE WOULD LIKE TO HAVE FORGOTTEN THEM." "TIMES AND SEASONS," VOL. 1, Pg. 81, ELDERS JOURNAL, Pg. 59, SENATE DOCUMENT, 139, Pg. 6, 9.**

Also, History of the Church, Vol. 3, pg. 232. Joseph Smith brands these three men, his three main witnesses to the Book of Mormon, "thieves and liars," and then asks us to believe their "testimony," about the Book of Mormon!

32. **DID YOU KNOW THAT MURDER IS AN UNFORGIVABLE SIN? JOSEPH SMITH SAID SO, IN DOCTRINE AND COVENANTS 42:18; 132:26, 27.**

Yet David and Saul/Paul, both murdered and were forgiven, Acts 9:1, Acts 22:4, II Sam. 12:13. The Bible clearly declares that, ". . . the blood of Jesus Christ, His Son, cleanseth us from *all* sin." I John 1:7

33. **DID YOU KNOW THE BIBLE SAYS WE CAN KNOW FALSE PROPHETS BY THEIR FRUITS. (NOT BY THEIR CLAIMS, FEELING, BURNING IN THE BOSOM OR "TESTIMONY").**

Doctrinally, we have tested the Mormon prophets.

Now let us consider the fruits of Mormonism in its heartland, Utah, which has ranged from almost totally Mormon to the present 72%. DID YOU KNOW THE DIVORCE RATE IN UTAH HAS TOPPED THE U.S. AVERAGE FOR ALL BUT 3 YEARS SINCE 1900!!?? Deseret News, Wednesday, February 11, 1976, reporting on one year, says *"Utah Divorces Top U.S. Average"* This *fact* hardly fits in with the "happiness is the family home evenings," "image," Mormons seek to create. DID YOU KNOW "UTAH TEEN SUICIDES LEAD U.S. AVERAGE", . . . "RATE AMONG UTAH TEENAGERS HAS CONSISTENTLY LED THE NATIONAL AVERAGE." Deseret News, September 3, 1979. DID YOU KNOW THAT THE SUICIDE RATE FOR UTAH WOMEN NEARLY DOUBLED FROM 1960 TO 1970? Deseret News, Friday, September 21, 1979. DID YOU KNOW THAT "SEVEN OUT OF EVERY TEN CHILDREN BORN TO TEENAGERS IN UTAH ARE CONCEIVED OUT OF WEDLOCK?" Ogden Standard-Examiner, Sat. Eve., December 15, 1979.

Not only that, but many authorities claim that there are as many as 30,000 polygamist, (tho' forbidden and outcast by the church), living in Utah, Arizona, etc., as a direct result of Joseph Smith's and Brigham Young's teaching on and practice of polygamy. These are the "fruits" of Mormonism, and all but the latter are easily verifiable facts. And this is just the tip of the iceberg. (For example, many Mormon wives are counseled to leave their husbands, to divorce them, if they will not become Mormons, or if they leave the Mormon Church! This is documented in the film, *"The God Makers."*)

## 34. DID YOU KNOW THAT THE GOSPEL AND TRUE CHRISTIANITY DISAPPEARED FROM OFF THE EARTH ABOUT THE FIRST CEN-

## TURY, UNTIL IT WAS "RESTORED" BY PROPHET SMITH IN 1830? MORMON THEOLOGY SAYS SO!

I Tim. 4:1 tells us that ". . . in the *latter* times SOME shall depart from the faith, giving heed to seducing spirits and doctrines of devils." The very existence of Mormonism and other groups totally different from Biblical Christianity certainly prove *that* to be true, and unwittingly, the Mormons have called themselves the *latter* day Saints, identifying themselves with those who in the *latter* times would depart from the faith! However, there is nowhere in the Bible or human experience a time of TOTAL APOSTASY, only SOME departed. Jesus plainly said the "gates of Hell would not prevail against His church" and He does not lie!! He also said He would be with His church continuously, always, which would have been impossible and futile if the church had disappeared as Joseph Smith and Mormon doctrine claims. Millions died at the stake, were burned to death, tortured, beaten, lived in caves and died for the Lord Jesus Christ during these hundreds of years Joseph Smith claimed the gospel, the church, and true Christianity had disappeared from the earth. Sixty-six million Christians are estimated to have died for their faith, singing hymns to Jesus while they burned or were torn asunder. Read of men like John Hus, and John Wycliffe, in history, or millions like them in Foxes' Book of Martyrs, and weep for the injustice done them by so foul a claim!! (Read the chapter on "The True Church," in "The Mormon Illusion," by Floyd C. McElveen). See Matt. 16:18—"Church,—Gates of Hell." Also Matt. 28:19-20.

Incidentally, beloved Mormon friends, let me address you personally for a moment! Please do not pass the facts in this book off as "lies, half-truths, distortions, statements out of context, etc." Do not compromise your integrity and insult the intelligence God gave you, with such shallow excuses. This is a common response of Mormons, as well as others in fatal error, who really have no other defense when God in His love reveals the truth to them. In your heart you know these facts are NOT lies, half-truths, distortions, or things taken out of context. I have met Mormons face to face with the facts recorded in this book, when they gave this kind of answer. They could not prove these claims, these incontrovertible facts, false, in any way whatsoever. Never claim something to be a lie or a half-truth unless you have thoroughly examined the eivdence and have irrefutable proof that it is false.

My heart aches for you, for the hurt you must feel. The answer to that hurt, however, is not to play spiritual ostrich and hide your head in the Mormon sand, avoiding the facts which can deliver your soul and those of your friends and loved ones. To deny the facts, to turn from God's light, to make false accusations to cover up, could forever doom your soul! The answer is to honestly face the facts, as thousands of Mormons are now doing, and turn from Mormonism to the Biblical Lord Jesus Christ!!

**35. DID YOU KNOW THAT MORMONS TEACH THAT ALL OTHER CHURCHES ARE FALSE? THAT THEY ARE ". . . ALL WRONG . . . ALL THEIR CREEDS WERE AN ABOMINATION IN HIS SIGHT; THAT THOSE PROFESSORS WERE CORRUPT. . ." JOSEPH SMITH, "PEARL OF GREAT PRICE," JOSEPH SMITH 2:18, 19.**

Naturally, Joseph Smith claimed that God said this . . . in no other way could he have established credibility for his "restored gospel." Joseph Smith (and Mormon doctrine) goes on to claim that the Mormon Church is the only true church on earth, and men can only reach the highest "heaven," degree of glory, exaltation, and/or become Gods, through the Mormon Church. Then the attack on other churches really began!! "ALL WILL BE DAMNED WHO ARE NOT LATTER-DAY SAINTS." Ora Pate Steward, "We Believe." "BOTH CATHOLICS AND PROTESTANTS ARE NOTHING LESS THAN THE 'WHORE OF BABYLON' WHOM THE LORD DENOUNCES BY THE MOUTH OF JOHN THE REVELATOR AS HAVING CORRUPTED ALL THE EARTH BY THEIR FORNICATIONS AND WICKEDNESS. ANY PERSON WHO SHALL BE SO WICKED AS TO RECEIVE A HOLY ORDINANCE OF THE GOSPEL FROM THE MINISTERS OF ANY OF THESE APOSTATE CHURCHES WILL BE SENT DOWN TO HELL WITH THEM, UNLESS THEY REPENT OF THE UNHOLY AND IMPIOUS ACT." Apostle Orson Pratt in "The Seer," pg. 255. For many years Mormon missionaries carefully maneuvered their potential convert to say, about all churches but the Mormon Church, including the church they might be a member of, "They are false." This was true in the August, 1961 Mormon Missionary Handbook, but has since been modified, but the basic thrust is the same. WOULD YOU BELIEVE, WHEN CHRISTIANS SIMPLY TRY TO ANSWER THIS, TO SHOW MORMONS THAT IT IS *THEIR* CHURCH WHICH IS WRONG, AND NOT THE HUNDREDS OF MILLIONS IN CHRISTIANITY EXPRESSING THEIR LOVE FOR GOD IN DIFFERENT CHURCHES, THE MORMONS FALL BACK ON, "WHY ARE YOU PERSECUTING MY CHURCH?" WE NEVER DO THAT TO ANY OTHER CHURCH!" Thank God, this is America, and even a condemned man has the right to defend himself. So do the millions of us who have been branded by Mormonism as being false or corrupt.

However, we have a far better motive for answering Mormons. We love them, and want to see them saved. Naturally, many will claim we hate them, we are persecuting them, Jesus would *never* do what we have done, etc. We understand that, and still love those who will respond this way. After all, what other defense, really, do they have? But some will listen, and look to the Saviour, and really be saved by the Biblical, not the Mormon, Christ, and *that* makes it worth it all!! Jesus was so loving and tender with any sinner, no matter how vile his sin. But Jesus was extremely stern with those who were religious but lost, *not* because he did not love them, but *because He did*! To the religious Pharisees, who fasted two whole days a week, tithed everything they owned, even down to the plants in their garden, belonged to the "one true" "church" (religious system God Himself had established), prayed long prayers and were zealous and sincere, but sincerely wrong, He declared: Matt. 23:15, "Woe unto you, scribes and Pharisees, hypocrites! For ye compass sea and land to make one proselyte, and when he is made, ye make him twofold more the child of Hell than yourselves." v. 27, "Woe unto you, scribes and Pharisees, for ye are like unto whited sepulchres which appear beautiful outward but are within full of dead men's bones, and of all uncleanness." In v. 33, Jesus says, "ye serpents, ye generation of vipers, how can ye escape the damnation of Hell."

Jesus loved these men enough to tell them the truth. He later died in brutal, bloody agony for them, as well as for all men, and some of them realized they were religious but lost, and turned to Him, among them Joseph of Arimathaea and Nicodemus.

Actually Brigham Young challenged us to test the Book of Mormon, and Mormonism, by Scripture, and Apostle Orson Pratt made this bold challenge: "This book must be either true or false, if false, it is one of the most cunning, wicked, bold, deep laid impositions ever palmed upon the world, calculated to deceive and ruin millions who will sincerely receive it as the Word of God, and will suppose themselves securely built upon the rock of truth until they are plunged with their families into hopeless despair. The nature of the message in the Book of Mormon is such that, if true, no one can possibly be saved and reject it; if false, no one can possibly be saved and receive it. Therefore, every soul in all the world is equally interested in ascertaining its truth of falsity . . . If after a rigid examination, it be found an imposition, it should be *extensively published* to the world as such; the evidences and arguments on which the imposture was detected, should be clearly and logically stated, that those who have been sincerely yet unfortunately deceived, may perceive the nature of the deception and be reclaimed, and that those who continue to publish the delusion, may be exposed and silenced . . . by evidences adduced from Scripture and reason." Orson Pratt, "Divine Authority of the Book of Mormon," introduction, a series of pamphlets published in 1850-51 quoted in, "The Book of Mormon—True or False?" Arthur Budvarson.

Any true Christian, who cares at all about the souls of men, Mormon or non-Mormon, about the Word of God, about the Lord Jesus Christ, must answer this challenge. Not to do so would confirm millions in their error, and encourage those who perpetrate that error, and deceive them into a lost eternity, all the while telling ourselves we love them too much to offend them!!! Actually, it is cowardice, not love, and direct disobedience to God's Word. Jude 3B . . . ". . . that ye should earnestly contend for the faith which was once delivered unto the saints." To be *contentious* is of the devil. To *contend* is of the Lord, honestly, lovingly, speaking the truth in love, weeping and praying for those who have been led astray, even as our Lord wept over "religious" Jerusalem.

If there are those who can lead more Mormons to Christ by simply telling them God loves them and presenting the positive gospel of Christ to them I am immeasurably thrilled! I say to them, *"Don't change, go to it, and God bless you!"* However, I have led scores of Mormons to Christ, but very few dedicated, knowledgeable Mormons UNTIL I FIRST REVEALED (AS GENTLY, BUT TRULY, AS POSSIBLE TO THEM) WHAT THEY WERE IN, AND EXACTLY HOW THEY HAD BEEN MISLED. (EVEN AS APOSTLE ORSON PRATT CHALLENGED US TO DO, AND THE BIBLE COMMANDS US TO DO, WHEN NECESSARY!) If some have a better method and it works, by all means use it! But God has graciously delivered hundreds of Mormons by the means I am using. The Mormon's problem is stated in Rom. 10:2 . . . "They have a zeal for God, but not according to knowledge." (See also Rom. 10:3, which *exactly* describes the Mormon!)

It is true that Matt. 7:1 tells HYPOCRITES not to judge, but John 7:23 tells CHRISTIANS to "judge righteous judgment."

As stated in "The Mormon Illusion," Floyd McElveen, "It is true that we should not major on minors. It may be unnecessary to tell our neighbor that he has bad breath, or that a shingle on his roof is loose. However, it is criminal not to wake him up if he is asleep inside his house and his house is on fire. No excuse, and no empty professions of love will ever satisfy God in such cases."

We hope this explains to individual Mormons that we are not persecuting them—we love them! What would you think of the man we just mentioned whose house is on fire with him asleep inside, if we ran into the burning building and woke him up, and he cried, "Leave me alone, why are you persecuting me?"

So help me God, as far as I know in my heart, we believe Mormons are lost and going to Hell, whether they believe it or not, and *love cannot do less* than to try to warn them and reach them for Christ. We love Mormons; not Mormonism. Just as Jesus loves the sinner, but NOT his sin!

Basically, there are four reasons Mormons need the Biblical Lord Jesus Christ and His salvation:

1. The God, (or Gods), of Mormonism is NOT the God of the Bible.

2. The Christ of Mormonism is NOT the Christ of the Bible.

3. The prophet of Mormonism is NOT a prophet of God.

4. The salvation of Mormonism is NOT the salvation of God.

This is dealt with carefully in "The Mormon Illusion," by Floyd McElveen, so we will briefly deal here with clear but short and simple answers, and present the Biblical plan of salvation.

And now, dear friends, we have arrived at the very heart of why this booklet has been written, beginning from here to the end of the booklet, truly. It is *"From Mormon Illusion to God's Love."*

# PART II

# THIS IS THE WAY

**Step 1.** ONE GOD. God loves you and wants you to know that there is only ONE GOD.

This ONE GOD created and is LORD over all the universe, stars, planets and all. Gen. 1:1. "In the beginning GOD created the heaven and earth."

Isaiah 43:10B . . . "Before me there was NO GOD FORMED, neither SHALL there be after me."

God was NEVER a man, and man will NEVER be GOD! As the eternal God he became the *God-man* Jesus, to die for us, but for all eternity he was God, not man.

Ps. 90:2B . . . "From everlasting (that's eternity past) to everlasting (that's eternity future) THOU ART GOD!

God never progressed, earned or attained His way to being God, HE WAS ALWAYS GOD. (The Bible mentions false gods, but to believe that other gods really exist is pagan polytheism, not Christianity.)

Clearly, there is not now, and NEVER will be, any other God on this planet or any other "world" or planet. There is forever only ONE God. Men *cannot* become Gods—none ever has, none ever will!

Isaiah 46:9B, . . . "For I am God, and there is none else; I am God, and there is none like me." Again— 43:10B . . . "Before me there was no God formed, neither shall there be after me!!!"

**Step 2.** ONE SAVIOUR, JESUS CHRIST, WHO IS ETERNALLY GOD.

Isaiah 9:6 . . . "For unto us a child is born, unto us a son is given, and the government shall be upon His shoulder, and His name shall be called wonderful, couselor, THE MIGHTY GOD, THE EVERLASTING FATHER, the Prince of Peace." Within the nature of God there are three eternal distinctions, God the Father, God the Son, and God the Holy Spirit, and there is only ONE God. Since Jesus is repeatedly called God, we MUST accept Him as God, or we accept another Jesus. In the Bible, the Word means Jesus (John 1:14) . . . "In the beginning was the *Word*, and the Word was with God, and THE WORD WAS GOD!" Beginning here simply means, "from all time." As God was God *from all time*, so was Jesus Christ God, FROM THE BEGINNING, FROM ALL TIME! Jesus never progressed, worked, or attained His way into being God, HE ALWAYS WAS GOD.

God forbade forever the worship of any other God, Ex. 34:14; yet Jesus accepted worship as God on many occasions. Matt. 28:9 . . . "And as they went to tell his disciples, behold Jesus met them, saying All Hail. And they came and held Him by the feet and WORSHIPPED HIM!" No wonder Thomas cried out to Jesus "my Lord and my God."

Unfortunately, Man has a sin-nature that separates him from true worship of God.

**Step 3.** ONE SIN-NATURE

An apple tree is an apple tree BEFORE it bears apples. it bears apples BECAUSE it is an apple tree.

So, we sin BECAUSE we have a sin-nature. An apple tree is just as much an apple tree by nature, whether it bears one apple or a thousand! So it is with a sinner.

One sin or a thousand is *not* the point! The point is, we *all* have a sin nature that *must be changed*.

Beating the apples off the tree does NOT change the nature of the tree! So, getting rid of some sins does not change our nature!

John 3:7 . . . "Ye MUST be born again." John 1:12 tells us how . . . "To as many as received Him to THEM gave He the power to BECOME the sons of God, even to them that BELIEVE on His name."

We are NOT by nature children of God. We must receive Christ in order to BECOME the children of God.

We are sinners by Nature and Choice. Sin is the fruit of our sin-nature, of each of us as sinners. Sin is "going our own way," Isaiah 53:6. It is being the God, Manager, Boss, Lord of our own life. It is being self-centered instead of Christ-centered.

Eph. 2:8 & 9 . . . "For by grace are ye saved through faith; and that not of yourselves: it is the gift of God: Not

BAPTISM  GOOD WORKS  {GOD}  NO!  "NOT BY WORKS" Eph 2:9

CHURCH  TITHES

of works, lest any man should boast." Rom. 3:10B . . . "there is NONE righteous, no not ONE."

Rom. 4:5-6 . . . "Now to Him that WORKETH (for salvation) is the reward not reckoned of grace, but of DEBT. But to Him that WORKETH NOT but BELIEVETH on Him that justifieth the UNGODLY, His FAITH is counted for righteousness.

Salvation is not by works, it is a GIFT. Personally receiving Christ, trusting Him alone to save us, is God's way of salvation.

Rom. 6:23 . . . "For the wages of sin is death, but the GIFT of God is eternal life through Jesus Christ, our Lord."

We cannot make ourselves "worthy" of the grace of God. Salvation is a free gift for the unworthy, the undeserving, which we all are. Christ died for the "ungodly" . . . Rom 5:6.

A dog does not bark in order to become a dog. He barks because he already is a dog. His barking helps demonstrate that fact! Just so, we do not do good works in order to become Christians (be saved). We do good works *after* we are saved (become Christians) to demonstrate the fact that we have been saved!

"All our righteousnesses are as filthy rags." . . . Isaiah 64:6B.

**Step 3.** ONE SIN-NATURE (CONT'D). We are sinners by nature and choice.

Rom. 3:23 . . . "For ALL have sinned and come short of the glory of God." This means we are all LOST sinners.

BESIDES
How much *Good Works*
can a *Dead* man do?

As natural men we are ALL,
"DEAD in trespasses and sins." Eph. 2:1B.

Although salvation is not by works, true salvation always produces a changed life. Christ comes in by personal invitation as Lord and Saviour to change our life, and live His life through us.

THE BLOOD OF JESUS CHRIST, GOD'S SON,
CLEANSES US FROM ALL SIN. I John 1:9

# TOO LATE / NOW

**Step 4.** ONE CHANCE.

II Cor. 6:2B . . . "Now is the accepted time, NOW is the day of salvation." There is NO chance after death. Heb. 9:27 . . . "And as it is appointed unto men once to die, but AFTER THIS THE JUDGMENT!" There is NO general salvation for all men because of Christ's death, but ONLY individual salvation for those who believe. John 3:36 . . . "He that *believeth* on the Son hath everlasting life; and he that BELIEVETH NOT THE SON SHALL NOT SEE LIFE: BUT THE WRATH OF GOD ABIDETH ON HIM!" All men are resurrected, but the unsaved dead are resurrected to DAMNATION, not salvation (John 5:29; Rev. 20:3-6)

Rev. 20:15 . . . "And whosoever was not found written in the book of life was cast into the lake of fire." Nowhere in the Bible is anyone EVER said to have been saved after they died. Today is the day of salvation.

Matt. 7:13 . . . "Enter in at the narrow gate; for wide is the gate, and broad is the way, that leadeth to destruction, and many there be who go in that way;"

Vs. 14 . . . "Because straight is the gate and narrow is the way, which leadeth unto life, and few there be that find it."

According to God's Word, the vast multitude of men are on the road to Hell, and to the resurrection unto damnation, John 5:29, unless they personally invite Christ into their life as Lord and Savior.

Death ends all hope for the lost.

SIN NATURE — SINNER

John 3:7 . . . "Ye MUST be born again."

Suppose a pig tried to become a sheep by ACTING like a sheep. Suppose the pig were clothed in sheep wool, ate sheep feed and even learned to bleat like a sheep. Would that *change* its pig nature and make it a sheep?

Would it matter whether or not the pig was "good" or "bad" by pig standards? So it is with trying to *act* like a Christian in order to become a Christian! It takes a miracle—the new birth.

## NEW NATURE — CHRISTIAN

**Step 5.** ONE WAY OF SALVATION.

Jesus alone can cleanse us from sin and change our nature. I Peter 2:24 . . . "Who His own self bare our sins in His own body on the tree."* Jesus took our place and shed His blood to cleanse us from sin. No amount of "good works" could wash away one sin or change our nature.

*Not just Adam's sin, but our own personal sins!

Salvation is instant. The moment we repent, turn from our sins to Jesus, He saves us. "Just as I am without one plea, but that the blood was shed for me."

Christ, to the unbaptized, unsaved, no good works, thief on the cross, in INSTANT salvation response to the thief's believing call; Luke 23:43B . . . "Today shalt thou be with me in paradise." (Same place Paul saw as the Heaven of God, I Cor. 12:2-4.) INSTANT salvation for a harlot. Luke 7:50B . . . "Go thy way, thy faith HATH

SAVED THEE!" INSTANT salvation in response to the publicans believing call. Luke 18:14A . . . "this man went down to his house justified."

Saul the murderer was changed to Paul the Apostle from one vital encounter with the living Christ.

Salvation includes accepting Jesus Christ as both Lord (*our* God, Lord, new manager) and Saviour. It involves heart (the ruling, governing, choosing, center of our being) belief. Rom. 10:9 . . . "That if thou shalt confess with thy mouth the Lord Jesus (Jesus as Lord) and shalt believe in thine HEART that God hath raised him from the dead, thou SHALT be saved.

We thus turn from our sins, our self, and our way to God's way. When we believingly call on the Lord Jesus Christ, He enters our life, cleanses us from sin, makes us children of God by the new birth, and gives us the free gift of salvation, with new, abundant, everlasting life. Heaven becomes our certain home, and His peace our possession.

There is no magic in the few puffs of air emitted from our vocal cords as we call on Christ. Yet He said, "Out of the abundance of the *heart* a man speaketh." If our call is from the heart, using our God-given power of choice to believe in Christ, *God Always Responds* and *Saves*! *He Promised!*

*Salvation is simple.* Rom. 10:13 . . . "For WHOSO-EVER shall CALL upon the name of the Lord, SHALL BE SAVED!"

We must personally CALL *believingly* on Jesus to save us. This is *how* we RECEIVE HIM. If we do so call, he MUST save us or God would be lying, and God CAN-NOT lie. If Jesus loved us enough to die in bloody agony to save us, would he then turn us down when we called on Him?

OF COURSE NOT!

"THE BLOOD OF JESUS CHRIST, GOD'S SON, CLEANSES US FROM ALL SIN." I John 1:9.

God loves you and wants you to be saved. Would you like to receive Jesus as your Lord and Saviour right now?

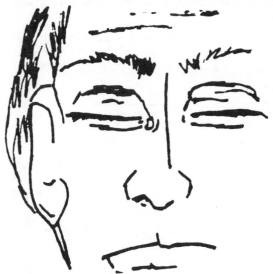

Just pray, if you mean it the best you know how, with all your heart.

"Lord Jesus Christ, come into my heart and life. Cleanse me from all sin by your shed blood. Make me a child of God. Give me your free gift of everlasting life, and let me know that I am saved, now and forever. I NOW receive you as my very own personal Lord and Saviour. In Jesus' name, amen."

Did Jesus save you or did He lie? He HAD to do one or other according to Rom. 10:13, if you called believingly on Him. Which did He do?

SALVATION IS CERTAIN

You can *know* you are saved, not just by *feeling*, but because God's Word says so! Memorize John 3:36A . . . *read it three times* . . . "He that believeth on the Son HATH everlasting life." What do you have right NOW according to God's Word? Where would you go if you were to die right now, according to God's Word?

If you KNOW that Jesus has saved you, according to His Word, please thank Him out loud for saving you as you pray.

I John 5:13A . . . "These things have I written unto you that believe on the name of the Son of God, that ye may KNOW that ye HAVE ETERNAL LIFE.

Choose to believe Christ, feelings or no feelings, and He will prove His reality to you as you step out on faith that He has kept His word and saved you. Three men step aboard an elevator bound for the third floor where they all want to go. One is laughing, one is crying, one is poker-faced, unemotional. All three of them get to the third floor, regardless of their feelings, because they BE-LIEVED the elevator would get them to the third floor, acted on their belief and committed themselves to the elevator. So it is with trusting Christ, feelings or no feelings.

The reality of your salvation will be shown in your love-response in obeying and following Jesus Christ. John 14:23A . . . "If a man love me, he WILL (not if, maybe and/or but) keep my words." If you are truly saved, you *will* obey!

To work FOR salvation shows UNBELIEF in the sufficiency of Jesus Christ alone to save us.

However, true salvation, true faith, ALWAYS PRO-DUCES good works! James 2:20 . . . "But wilt thou know, O vain man, that *faith without works is DEAD.*"

Apple trees do *not* have to produce apples in order to become an apple tree! Apples are products of the tree and prove that it is an apple tree. So, good works *never* produce a Christian, they merely *prove he is one.*

II Cor. 5:17 . . . "Therefore if any man is IN CHRIST, he is a NEW CREATION, old things are passed away; behold, all things are become new."

We must have salvation in order to *demonstrate* it, just as we must HAVE a car BEFORE we can demonstrate it!

True Christians Produce Good Works.

Find a church that makes salvation clear, that believes the Bible, and the Bible *alone*, that believes the blood of Christ alone can cleanse from sin. Attend church *faithfully*. Heb. 10:25 and I John 3:14. Follow Christ in baptism to picture your sins being washed away, AFTER you have been saved, Acts 10:47, 48 and to picture your death with Christ to the old life, and your resurrection with Him to new life. Pray daily, I Thess. 5:13, John 15:7. Confess sin instantly, I John 1:9. (A Christian can sin, but a true Christian cannot continue habitually in sin. I John 3:9.) Read the Bible daily, Acts 17:11, I Peter 2:2.

Confess Christ publically. Luke 12:8-9.

Share Christ with others constantly. Acts 1:8.

Begin memorizing at least a verse a week. Thank God every day that Jesus has saved you and thank Him for all things, good and bad. I Thess. 5:18.

Obey Him, believe Him, feelings or no feelings, by faith.

Believe Him for His victory, thank Him and step out on faith and He will prove His victory in your experience.

**Step 6.** ONE HEAVEN.

John 14:3 . . . "And if I go and prepare *A* place (one ONLY, not THREE), I will come again and receive you unto myself . . . that where I (JESUS) am, THERE ye may be also!" Matt. 13:24 . . . "And then shall He send His angels and shall GATHER TOGETHER His elect, from the four winds, from the uttermost part of the earth to the uttermost part of heaven." I Thess. 4:16-17 . . . "For the Lord Himself shall descend from heaven with a shout, with the voice of the archangel, and with the Trump of God; and the dead in Christ shall rise first; then we which are alive and remain shall be caught up together with them in the clouds, to meet the Lord in the air, and so shall we ever be with the Lord."

Jesus will be in the HIGHEST HEAVEN, the ONLY Heaven of God, and all his people will be with Him forever.

The Heaven of God is sometimes called the third heaven, to distinguish it from the other two heavens, one of the stars and planets, and one of the clouds and atmosphere.

This third heaven is the ONLY Heaven of God, and all the church-age saints will be with Him forever in heaven. It is where both Paul and the thief on the cross

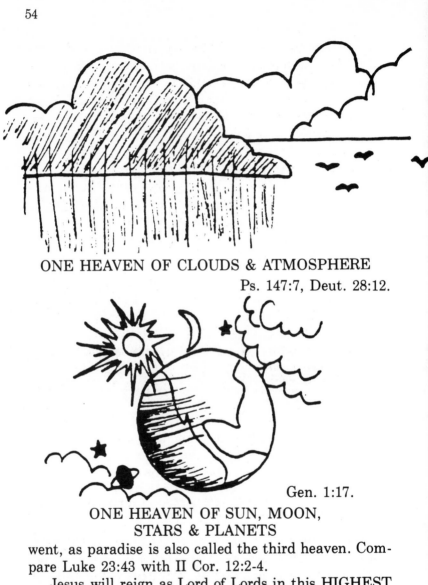

ONE HEAVEN OF CLOUDS & ATMOSPHERE

Ps. 147:7, Deut. 28:12.

Gen. 1:17.

ONE HEAVEN OF SUN, MOON,
STARS & PLANETS

went, as paradise is also called the third heaven. Compare Luke 23:43 with II Cor. 12:2-4.

Jesus will reign as Lord of Lords in this HIGHEST HEAVEN, the ONE Heaven of God, and all true Christians will be with Him forever.

Christian families will be together forever, *not* separated on different planets as "Gods."

Since in heaven we will be one family in Christ, and since He is called our heavenly bridegroom desiring and deserving our fullest love and adoration, marriage and reproduction there have forever ceased. Matt. 22:30 . . . "For in the resurrection they neither *marry*, nor are given in marriage, but are as ANGELS OF GOD in heaven." God is clearly saying here that there is NO MARRIAGE, and NO STATE OF BEING MARRIED in heaven, as we will be like the angels there. The angels of God are always mentioned in the masculine gender. They are NOT married, there are no "angel babies," being born in heaven. Sex in the human sense is not mentioned of them.

ONE HEAVEN
GOD Isa 66:1

### TO THOSE WHO HAVE JUST ACCEPTED CHRIST!

To wait for feeling to believe Christ is to deny faith. Feeling will come in God's time, however AFTER you have chosen by your *will* to believe God's Word and fully trust, commit yourself to, Christ. Salvation includes joy, but only AFTER the will has chosen Him by faith.

Let Jesus live His life through you, that's true Christianity. Share Christ by life and lip. God's purpose is now yours. Reach the lost at any cost. Acts 1:8, Luke 19:10, John 20:21.

Lay aside anything in your life that would hinder you, shame Christ, or cause others to stumble. *He* is your victory, I Cor. 15:57, Gal. 5:16. Surrender daily to the Holy Spirit's control of your life.

Finally, begin THIS SUNDAY a life of faithfulness to Christ by attending a gospel preaching church. We do not decide Monday morning whether we are going to work or not, that is a settled conclusion. Neither, if we are really serious Christians (neither deceiving ourselves or being deceived), do we decide on Sunday morning whether or not we are going to church. If we truly love Jesus that was settled forever when we committed our lives to Him. Now we *Follow Him*!

REMEMBER:

To work FOR salvation shows UNBELIEF in the sufficiency of Jesus Christ alone to save us.

However, true salvation, true faith, ALWAYS PRODUCES good works! James 2:20 . . . "But wilt thou know, O vain man, that faith without works is DEAD."

Write: Ed Decker
℅ SAINTS ALIVE IN JESUS
P.O. Box 1076
Issaquah, WA 98027
For further information or help.


HIGHLY RECOMMENDED READING:
"MORMONISM, SHADOW OR REALITY," Jerald & Sandra Tanner
"MORMON CLAIMS ANSWERED," Marvin Cowan
"TO MORONI WITH LOVE," Ed Decker
" THE MORMON ILLUSION," Floyd McElveen

See the film: "THE GOD MAKERS"
     Floyd C. McElveen
     6795 Phillips Road
     Port Orchard, WA 98366
     (Sketches by Ginger Lake—Some based on
     originals by Karen Davis)
    (This book is designed to be used both as a witnessing tool and a give away tract. A *much shorter* condensed version is also being made available.)

Beloved Mormon friends, a great exodus is beginning to take place from the Mormon church. At the very time when Mormons have recently doubled in number, God is beginning to work in His great love and power. The "You took it out of context," "Why do you teach such lies about Mormonism?", "Why are you persecuting us?" excuses have worn thin for many heart-hungry Mormons. The context references from Mormon sources are given and many intelligent Mormons are checking them out and finding what we say is not "out of context," but exactly what their leaders taught, said, and did. Only dishonest people would claim something is out of context unless they have fully checked out the context the statement comes from; otherwise, it is only a shallow excuse which honest Mormons will not use. In just the last several years, thousands have turned to Christ through "Saints Alive in Jesus," "Ex-Mormons for Jesus," and "Concerned Christians," and also through books such as "Mormonism, Shadow or Reality," "The Mormon Illusion," "Mormon Claims Answered," "To Moroni With Love," and other books and tracts. Now the dynamite new film on Mormonism, "The God Makers," holds promise of turning additional thousands from Mormonism to Christ. Some, of course, and we say this with real tears, will never believe, having their minds blinded by Satan. Others have hardened their hearts until God has sent them "strong delusion that they should believe a lie, that they all might be damned who believed not the truth . . ." II Thess. 2:11-12. However, Mormonism shows definite signs of crumbling, and we plead with you, Mormon friends, if you value your soul, if you really care about your loved ones, if you really want true salvation, turn to the Biblical Christ and away from Mormonism while there is yet time.

Use scores of these little booklets, "From Mormon Illusion to God's Love," to reach your Mormon friends and families. Use the powerful book God is using worldwide to win Mormons and others to Christ—"The Mormon Illusion." See the film, "The God Makers," and get as many Mormon and other friends to see it as you can. The hour is late, the need is urgent. In the name of Jesus, I beseech you, please act now!

Floyd C. McElveen

# PART III

# THE CHRIST CHANGED LIFE
## John 14:23
# NEW LIFE DISCIPLESHIP
## FOLLOW-UP

1. Be baptized. Acts 2:41, 16:31-33, Acts 10:47-48.
2. Confess Christ before men. Luke 12:8-9, Rom. 10:9-10.
3. Attend church faithfully. Heb. 10:25, I John 3:14.
4. Read the Bible daily . . . Study it . . . Memorize special verses. I Peter 2:2, II Tim. 2:15, Ps. 1:2, 119:1, Joshua 1:8, Col. 3:16-17.
5. Pray daily. I Thess. 5:17, Jeremiah 33:3, Rom. 8:32, Matt. 18:19, 21:22, I John 5:14-15.
6. Confess sin instantly. Proverbs 28:13, I John 1:9.
7. Share Christ . . . Witness . . . Win the lost. Acts 1:8, Proverbs 11:30, Luke 5:10, 19:10, John 20:21, Psalms 126:6.
8. Let Jesus live His life through you. I Cor. 15:57, Col. 3:1-4, Gal. 2:20, 5:16. Live not by feeling, but by faith. Faith-root, feeling-fruit.

## DECISION, PLEASE

The definite decision for Christ is necessary and important. Life or death, Heaven or Hell, hinge upon this decision. That is why we stress the need of crystallizing belief into a concrete act of accepting Christ. We are told in the Bible to call, to receive, to be born again, to open the door.

Agrippa believed the prophets, Paul said, but was not a Christian; he did not personally receive the risen Christ. The devils believe and temble, God says, but they are doomed to Hell forever. Obviously then, there is a belief which falls short of saving faith in Christ, short of the act of receiving Him as Saviour and Lord, unconditionally.

A young man can love a young woman and she can return that love; yet they can remain apart in deepest frustration and sorrow until death. They do not belong to each other until in the simple act of marriage each consents to receive the other and forsake all others. So it is with Christ. One may profess to believe in Him, to love Him, and yet never receive Him, call on Him, open the door to Him for salvation. Saving faith then requires the act of calling on and receiving Christ and being born into the family of God. Then we are new creatures with new desires, new power, and new life (II Cor. 5:17).

Regardless then of how much we convince ourselves we love Him and believe in Him, we must call on Him, receive Him, open the door to Him, invite Him in by a definite decision or act of faith as the Bible says. Rom. 10:13 . . . "For whosoever shall call upon the name of the Lord shall be saved."

## HOW TO DO IT

If you are willing to make this definite decision for Christ right now, you may pray after this manner:

"Dear God, I confess that I am a sinner. I believe that you sent your Son to die on the cross for my sins. I want to receive Jesus into my heart, and I do open my heart and life to Him right now. Dear Jesus, come into my life and be my Lord and Saviour."

To further nail down this definite decision, you may wish to sign your name to the following statement:

I have today received Jesus Christ as my Lord and Saviour. I am claiming by faith His promise of sins forgiven and His gift of eternal life.

Signed: _____

Date: _____

## WELCOME TO GOD'S FAMILY

Congratulations! You have just become a child of God! You have just been born-again, born from above, born of the Spirit of God into the forever family of God! You are a new creation in Christ. Your sins are washed away by His shed blood. You have a new future, a new family, and a new Father! We have just shown you from God's Word how you can be saved and know it for sure from Rom. 10:13, John 3:36, and I John 5:13 (We suggest you memorize these verses). You can rejoice with all your heart that Jesus is yours and you are His forever, that Heaven and not Hell is your eternal home, and that He will be with you in a new and vital way now and forever. Salvation is instant, the results last forever!

Choose to believe Christ, feelings or no feelings, and He will prove His reality to you as you step out on faith that He has kept His word and saved you, when you called believingly on Him. Rom. 10:13 . . . "For whosoever shall call upon the name of the Lord shall be saved." Since God cannot lie, you can now KNOW that Jesus has saved you, according to God's Word.

**NOTE: This important illustration
one more time!**

Three men step aboard an elevator bound for the

third floor where they all want to go. One is laughing, one is crying, one is pokerfaced, unemotional. All three of them get to the third floor, regardless of their feelings, because they BELIEVED the elevator would get them to the third floor, acted on their belief, and COMMITTED THEMSELVES to the elevator. So it is with trusting Christ, feelings or no feelings.

The reality of your salvation will be shown in your love-response in obeying and following Christ. John 14:23 . . . ". . . if a man love me, he WILL (not if, maybe, and/or but!) keep my words." If you are truly saved, you *will* obey! Clearly, obedience does not save you, or help you get saved, or help you stay saved. Eph. 2:8, 9 . . . "For by grace are ye saved through faith; and that *not* of yourselves; it is the *gift* of God; *not of works*, lest any man should boast."

Just as clearly, the love-response to Christ of good works, because of gratitude and love, because of His new life in you, will flow from you when truly saved. James says cogently, James 2:20 . . . "But wilt thou know, O vain man, that faith without works is dead?" Titus warns also, Titus 1:16 . . . "They profess that they know God; but in works they deny Him, being abominable, and disobedient, and unto every good work reprobate." Jesus gave a parable in Luke 8:5-18 which speaks powerfully to these shallow head, but not heart believers, also. Read it!!!

Finally, Heb. 6:9 unequivocally states, "But, beloved, we are persuaded better things of you, and things that accompany salvation though we thus speak."

To sum up: To work FOR salvation shows unbelief in the sufficiency of Jesus Christ alone to save you. However, true salvation, true faith always produces good works. An apple tree is an apple tree before it ever produces an apple. It produces apples because it *already is* an apple tree, *never* in order *to become* an apple tree. So it is with the Christian, good works demonstrate the salvation we already have. Obedience is the proof that we have been saved, our love-response to our Saviour, the evidence of the new life now dwelling in us, and enables us to grow in Him.

As II Cor. 5:17 declare . . . "Therefore if any man be in Christ, he is a new creature; old things are passed away; behold, all things are become new." How delightful! How exciting!

Now let me share with you how to begin and continue with your new life of love-response, obedience and growth in Christ. As a real child of God, I know you will be ready to obey the Lord Jesus Christ, just as God's Word says you will in John 14:23.

## 1. BE BAPTIZED

The waters of baptism cannot wash away one sin. That was done the moment you were saved by the shed blood of the Lord Jesus Christ. But God commanded that we be baptized as soon as we have been saved. Just as the approximately 3,000 converts in Acts 2:41 were baptized the day they were saved, and the jailer in Philippi was baptized the very night he believed and was saved, Acts 16:31-33, so we should be baptized as soon as possible after we are saved. Baptism is an outward picture of an inward cleansing by the blood of Christ. It comes after salvation; before salvation it has no value or meaning. It pictures on the outside what Christ has already done on the inside. Even more important, Biblically, it pictures our death to the old life with Jesus, identifies us with His death for us, identifies us with His burial for us as we go down under the water of Baptism, and identifies us with His risen life as we rise from the water of Baptism as He bodily arose from the grave. We are thus publically forever declaring our identification with the Lord Jesus Christ, our death to the old life, and declaring our new life in Him. Acts 10:47, 48, clearly shows the order, salvation, then baptism. See also Rom. 6:1-4.

Baptism is by immersion since that is exactly what the original word meant, and since that alone fulfills the picture of death, burial, and resurrection which the Bible presents as a picture of our identification with Christ.

Stated another way, when we have been saved, God counts it that we died with Christ in His death, were buried with Him, and rose with Him to new life. Baptism pictures this! Beautiful! *Do it*, not in order to be saved, but because you have *already* been saved, and now want to fully love and obey Him!!

## 2. CONFESS CHRIST BEFORE MEN

Luke 12:8, 9 . . . "Also I say unto you, whosoever shall confess me before men, him shall the Son of man also confess before the angels of God: But he that denieth Me before men shall be denied before the angels of God."

Open, public confession of Jesus Christ is Biblical evidence and confirmation of salvation. That is why many of our churches give public invitations so that before a friendly, loving crowd praying for just such miracles, you may acknowledge Christ. *God* commanded confession before men. If those early disciples in Jerusalem had declared that salvation was a private thing between them and God only, and had refused to confess God before men, often hostile, murderous men, the gospel would never have spread beyond Jerusalem, and we would be on our way to Hell without a Saviour! So *confess Christ before men*, in church as a good beginning, and wherever God leads. It is tremendously strengthening!

## 3. ATTEND CHURCH FAITHFULLY

Heb. 10:25 . . . "Not forsaking the assembling of ourselves together, as the manner of some is, but exhorting one another; and so much the more, as ye see the day approaching." "Assembly" and "church" have virtually the same meaning in this context, so God is saying not to forsake the "churching" of ourselves together. The New Testament knows nothing of a true Christian living in isolation from the local church. We immediately become part of the body of Christ upon our salvation. Each of us have gifts to share with one another; we form different but essential parts of the body of Christ. We attend church both to give and receive. God gave godly men with special gifts to serve the church, officers called pastors to oversee and feed us, and deacons also. He carefully created the church, and gave special ordinances to the church, Baptism and the Lord's Supper. He is not about to ignore His beloved church, and meet with some disobedient Christian gone A.W.O.L. in the woods or in some "spiritual" fellowship that bypasses His church. Frankly, to despise the local church is to despise the Lord of the local church, whether one is aware of it or not. The Bible says that Christ is the head of the church, and the church is His body. Just as it would be nonsense to marry a person's head and have nothing to do with their body, so it would be nonsense to "marry" Christ, (be joined to Him eternally through conversion) and have nothing to do with His body, the church. It is true that there are sometimes hypocrites in the church, but that only proves the Bible true, for Christ predicted such in

His parable of the tares and wheat. He will tend to that in due time.

The thrilling thing is that you are now a part of the family of God, filled with brothers and sisters with whom you will spend eternity! Sharing their joys and burdens, being discipled to be more and more like Jesus Christ, to His glory!!

So, ATTEND CHURCH FAITHFULLY! This is one of the surest evidences that you have truly been saved. I John 3:14 . . . "We know that we have passed from death unto life, because we LOVE the brethren . . ." If we love Jesus and the brethren we will be delighted to be with them in church.

Be sure to find a church that clearly believes the Bible, and the Bible only, to be the inspired, infallible Word of God. Find a church that believes that Jesus Christ's blood cleanses from sin and that depends on Him alone for salvation.

## 4. READ THE BIBLE DAILY

I Peter 2:2 . . . "As newborn babes, desire the sincere milk of the Word, that ye may grow thereby." As food is to you physically, so the Word of God is to you now spiritually. Ask God to help you understand each time you read it, and He will. Start with the gospel of John, then read I John, then the New Testament, and then the Old Testament. God's Word gives growth, strength, helps you to avoid sin, (Psalms 119:11), illuminates your daily walk with God, brings peace, knowledge and wisdom, heightens joy, and lessens danger. Joshua 1:8, Psalms 1:2, Col. 3:16-17. If possible, it is best to read your Bible and pray early in the morning before facing the day, just as it is best to tune your instruments before playing in the orchestra; but anytime is acceptable. It has been well said, "This book will keep you from sin, or sin will keep you from this book." *Memorize special verses!* (See also II Tim. 2:15.)

## 5. PRAY DAILY . . . AND MORE OFTEN!

I Thess 5:17 . . . "Pray without ceasing." You now have a hot-line to heaven through the Lord Jesus Christ. God *promises* to answer prayer. (Jeremiah 33:3, Matt. 18:19, Matt. 21:22, I John 5:14-15) Reading the Bible is God talking to you, prayer is you talking to God (tho' He speaks to your heart as you pray, also) and witnessing is your talking for God. Praise God, worship Him, thank Him, and ask Him for your needs believingly every day. *Very important:* tell the Lord Jesus Christ, preferably out loud, every day, that you love Him and thank Him for dying on the cross for you and giving you eternal life. It is amazing what this will do for you and for Him, in warmth, love, and abiding fellowship. (*It turns your mountains into molehills!*)

Together, prayer and Bible-study form the essence of our communication with Jesus. Love in its practical application is spelled T-I-M-E. The quintessence of our love for God is expressed and enhanced by the time we spend with Him in prayer and Bible-study. Those who profess to have no time for prayer and Bible-study may call into questions the reality of their relationship with Jesus Christ. A person claiming that he has no time for Bible-study, for prayer, to live for God, is like a bird declaring that it has no time to fly, or a fish claiming it has no time to swim. For this, they were created. To love God, spend time with Him, get to really know Him and serve Him, for this, we were created. At the very least, neglect insures leanness of soul, defeat and heartbreak instead of triumph and joy. Through prayer and Bible-study we tap God's love and power, and grow into mature Christians established in doctrine and practice, and most of all Christlikeness. The fruit of the Spirit, love, joy, peace, longsuffering, gentleness, goodness, faith, meekness, temperance, will flow from us to His glory and attract others to Him! Besides, what a thrill it is to see the God of the universe answering your prayers.

It is probably true that no Christian is any stronger, or better, or greater, than his prayer life! It is doubtful if anything worthwhile has ever been accomplished except by prayer . . . often much prayer. Even as a new babe in Christ, like the first call of a baby to its mother, your prayers are very precious to God. Begin the habit of prayer and Bible-study right now. Perhaps the greatest reward of all is that, as you daily focus in on Christ through prayer and Bible-study, you become like Him! II Cor. 3:18. As a plant looks to the sun and is transformed by photosynthesis, so let us look to Jesus in prayer and Bible-study, and we will be transformed into His likeness by Christosynthesis! Christ now actually dwells in you and intercedes for you! Pray in confidence and boldness in His name.

## 6. CONFESS SIN INSTANTLY . . . HONESTLY . . . AND AVOID IT!

Prov. 28:13 . . . "he that covereth his sins shall not prosper; but whosoever confesseth and forsaketh them shall have mercy." Christians can still sin, because although we have a new nature, we still have the old nature, but God has made provision in Christ. I John 1:9 . . . "If we confess our sins, He is faithful and just to forgive us our sins, and to cleanse us from all unrighteousness." Instant confession, of the thought before the deed is done, avoids much sorrow and heartbreak, but thought or deed should be confessed to God, for instant forgiveness and virtually unbroken fellowship, turning by His strength from that which caused us to stumble. Remember, a Christian can sin, but a true Christian cannot live in sin.

*First,* because when we came to Christ, we repented of our sins (changed our minds about sin, self and the Saviour) turning from self and sin as the Lord of our life (Rom. 10:9 . . . "That if thou shalt confess with thy mouth the Lord Jesus [literally, *Jesus* as *Lord*], and shalt believe in thine heart that God hath raised Him from the dead, thou shalt be saved.") *Secondly,* because, though we are sometimes surprised by sin, I John 3:9 tells us, "Whosoever is born of God doth not commit (habitually practice or continue in, literally) sin." To illustrate, a pig and a sheep could be taken, washed, perfumed, beribboned, petted and kept in one's home. But if someone left the door open, the pig would head for the first mudhole and wallow happily in it; that is the pig nature. The sheep might fall into the same mudhole, (I've seen some very dirty sheep), but would get out as quickly as possible. It is not a sheep's nature to wallow happily in a mudhole, even though it might fall into it, and so it is with the true Christian. He can never again wallow happily in sin, and will seek to flee from temptation, to avoid sin, but he can still sin. *Thirdly,* we are told, I John 2:15 . . . "Love not the world (not speaking of trees, birds, etc. but the wicked world system presided over by Satan) neither the things that are in the world. If any man love the world, the love of the Father is not in him." Sin and the world are what Jesus saved us from. There is no point in going back into them any more than there would be for Lazarus to crawl back into the tomb, after Jesus raised him from the dead, to have fellowship with rotting corpses. The Bible says we have passed "from death to life," and these are the things of death. Nevertheless, when we do sin, instant confession and instant forgiveness are the answer. Sonship can never be broken; fellowship can, and sin breaks fellowship between us and God. Agreeing with God about our sin honestly in confession instantly restores that sweet fellowship. (See God's promise in 1 Cor. 10:13!)

## 7. WITNESS . . . SHARE CHRIST WITH OTHERS . . . WIN THE LOST!

Acts 1:8 . . . "But ye shall receive power, after that the Holy Ghost is come upon you; and ye shall be witnesses unto me both in Jerusalem, and in all Judea, and in Samaria, and unto the uttermost part of the earth." Also, Matt. 4:19 . . . "And He saith unto them, 'Follow me, and I will make you fishers of men.' " (Those not fishing, call into question the reality of their following, obviously.) We are saved to be conformed to the image of Christ, to bring glory to Him. However, the very heart of this is sharing Christ and winning others to Him. *Purpose* . . . Luke 5:10B . . . ". . . from henceforth thou shalt CATCH men. (Actually WIN them, NOT just fish for them.) *Promise* . . . "He that goeth forth and weepeth, bearing precious seed shall doubtless come again rejoicing, bringing his sheves (the *harvest, souls*) with him." Prov. 11:30 . . . "The fruit of the righteous is a tree of life; and he that winneth souls is wise." See Dan. 12:3, and Ezek. 33:8. *Priority* . . . Luke 19:10 . . . "For the Son of Man is come to seek and save that which was lost." His Priority and Purpose . . . John 20:21 . . . "Then said Jesus to them again, 'Peace be unto you; AS THE FATHER HAS SENT ME, EVEN SO SEND I YOU.' " . . . now becomes our Priority and Purpose! May we also, by His loving grace, be consumed as was Paul, with his passion for the Lost . . . for His great heaviness and continual heart sorrow, caused Him to cry out, Rom. 9:3 . . . "For I could wish that myself were accursed from Christ for my brethren, my kinsmen according to the flesh."

Winning souls!! . . . THIS is the one thing we can do to make Jesus and the angels of Heaven rejoice! (Luke 15:9-10) There is also the rejoicing in the hearts of those reached for Christ, and the rejoicing in our own hearts, and in the church!

God's command and Christ's love within compel us to witness and win souls to our Savior. Also, more souls being saved, more people being conformed to His image, brings *more glory to Him*. Other motives: the joy of sharing good news, seeing messed-up lives transformed and made abundant here and now in this life, desire to share heaven with as many as possible, the growth and joy that occurs in oneself as we witness and share Him, the demonstration of the power and compassion of Christ, and last but not least, *saving precious lost souls from the awfulness of an eternity in the lake of fire*!! Truly, if salvation is the most important thing ever to happen to us, and it is, and if we "Love our neighbors as ourselves" as God commands, then love constrains us to share Christ with them to deliver them from sin and Hell. This is the most wonderful privilege and purpose known to man, sharing Christ, and winning the lost to glorify Him forever!

Begin by sharing what Christ has done for you and tell those to whom you witness how it can happen to them. Share the Bible verses that brought you salvation and assurance in Christ. You will become more and more effective as you revel in His love, learn His word, and share Him more and more with others.

# 8. LET JESUS LIVE HIS LIFE THROUGH YOU!

I Cor. 15:57 . . . "But thanks be to God which giveth us the victory through our Lord Jesus Christ." We cannot live the Christian life in our strength, He clearly said, "without me ye can do nothing," but we can live it in HIS strength. Letting Jesus daily live His life through you, being filled and controlled by His Holy Spirit, Eph. 5:18, takes much of the strain out of Christian life. Thus we can, Rom. 6:11 . . . ". . . reckon ye also yourselves to be dead indeed unto sin, but alive unto God through Jesus Christ our Lord." And we can, Gal. 5:16 . . . ". . .Walk in the Spirit, and ye shall not fulfill the lust of the flesh." We are NOT to live by feelings, but by FAITH, and as we step out on God's Word, feelings or not, we will find His Word true, His presence real, and the feelings ultimately will follow, as the *fruit*, never the *root* of our Christian life. The surrender mentioned in Rom. 12:1-2 is the reasonable step for a serious Christian, and Rom. 8:28 will leap to life and make I Thess. 5:18 its expression! Now that you are His, bought by His blood, give Him cheerfully and willingly, *first*, yourself, *followed* by your time, talents and treasure (tithes and offerings), Mal. 3:10, I Cor. 16:1-2. Love is the compelling motive in the Christian life, not legalism, which can be a slavish, mechanical obedience to stated laws out of fear or force, bringing constraint and unhappiness.

Thus a young wife could obey a list of rules posted daily by her husband. Yet love, a higher motive, an inner response to share and/or surrender to someone else for their good, would cause the young wife to seek ways to please her husband, rules or no rules, and something he expressed that she knew would please him would bring joyous response. This response would be done in complete freedom and bring happiness and peace. So it is with the Christian and Christ. Obeying is not legalism, it is the *attitude*, the motive, toward rules, toward obedience, which determines that. We cannot merit growth, but we can cease to hinder His love working in us by obeying rather than disobeying. Some have stretched the grace of God to cover living in disobedience to Him. It is true that God loves us as much when we fail as He did before we failed, and that is wonderful!! It is also true that when I picked up my babies because I loved them, if they had a dirty diaper, I did not love them less, nevertheless, I hastened to change the diaper, and so does God. He does not, He cannot leave us in the state in which He found us. Those who turn back—never real— are covered in I John 2:19 and Luke 8:5-18. *READ!!*

This is what the true grace of God, the unmerited favor, the free flow of His marvelous love on undeserving sinners REALLY does ... Titus 2:11-14 ... "For the grace of God that bringeth salvation hath appeared to all men, teaching us that, DENYING UNGODLINESS AND WORDLY LUST, WE SHOULD LIVE SOBERLY, RIGHTEOUSLY, AND GODLY, IN THIS PRESENT WORLD, looking for that blessed hope, and the glorious appearing of the great God and our Saviour Jesus Christ; who gave Himself for us, that He might redeem us from all iniquity, and purify unto himself a peculiar people zealous of good works."

Beloved, when you met Jesus, you met the Living God, for He *is* God. He is risen bodily, He is alive, and He is God. John 20:28, I Tim. 3:16. He is now your life. Col. 3 :1-4. He can meet all your needs. Phil. 4:13, 19; I Peter 5:7; John 14:1-3, 27.

The shimmering splendor of His life, new life, eternal life, is yours forever! Love His people, love the Word, and love the lost for Him! God bless you! I John 5:13.

## LAST WORDS IN HIS LOVE

Many Christians have found their lives gloriously transformed by Christ. He has fulfilled their deepest needs, calmed their fears, curbed their restlessness, taken away their guilt, lifted their burdens, given them His sweet and abiding peace. Their life is full and abundant, they revel in His love, they enjoy the Christian life, and love other Christians. Jesus is all in all to them, His life is now their life, and they love it.

Many others, unfortunately, though they say the same things about Jesus, claim they know Him, and love Him, are still wallowing most of the time, or much of the time, in the slough of despond. They are still restless, unfulfilled, often swallowed up in troubles, bad habits, sin, self-pity, barely able to keep their heads above water in the Christian life, much less bring any glory to Christ, grow, mature and be faithful as Christians, lead others to Christ, or be real pillars (pillows, maybe!) . . . in the church.

Some, of course, have never been truly saved, profession or not. However, many others are like a person who goes to the doctor, gets a prescription, with eight ingredients in it, and scratches out one or several of the ingredients before he gives it to the druggist to be filled. Then, after less than desirable, or even disasterous results, he blames the doctor or the druggist for the medicine not working. He may even lose faith in the doctor, or claim he is a fraud. Tragically, some do this in the Christian life. We must do what the great physician prescribes to enjoy and grow successfully in the Christian life. Love, loving Jesus, is the bottom line, but we must not take lightly II John 6a . . . "And this is love, that we walk after his commandments."

    1. Victory is a gift basically, as salvation was. II Cor. 15:57.

2. Know that you are dead to sin. Rom. 6:11. (Sin is NOT dead to you!)

3. Yield yourself to Jesus as one alive from the dead. Rom. 12:1-2.

4. Believe, accept, reckon, rely on, claim, and live these facts by FAITH not FEELING.

5. This is all true because of your identification with Christ in His death, burial and resurrection.

6. Claim His control, the filling of His Holy Spirit, by faith. Gal. 5:16, 2:20.

We must exercise the power of the Holy Spirit in our lives by faith. While He provides the power WE do it, by faith that He is working in and through us. As Ryrie well said, "God's working is not suspended because I work; neither is God's working always apart from my working." God bless you in your new life.!

Perhaps the greatest secret of that new life is to really believe and claim Rom. 8:28 and to *show that* confidence in Christ constantly. How? Practice always the following verse by faith, not feeling—for all things "good" and "bad":

I Thess. 5:18 . . . *"In everything give thanks, for this is the will of God in Christ Jesus concerning you."*

For information or help, or to share your decision, write:

Ed Decker
SAINTS ALIVE IN JESUS
P.O. Box 1076
Issaquah, WA 98027

"From Mormon Illusion to God's Love" was written by Floyd C. McElveen. He is also the Author of *"THE MORMON ILLUSION,"* a best-selling book God is using worldwide to reach Mormons and others for Christ.

However, as the national evangelist for the Conservative Baptist Home Mission Society, he is on the road a lot, and does not have the staff or Mormon material for further, in-depth follow-up such as his good friend, Ed Decker, has. Please write Ed first—unless you simply want to share your decision for Christ with McElveen, which would be a total joy to him!

Floyd C. McElveen
6795 Phillips Road S.E.
Port Orchard, WA 98366

77450